Partners in Prayer

Advent 2015

Copyright ©2015 by Christian Board of Publication, 483 E. Lockwood Ave., Suite 100, St. Louis, MO, 63119. No part of this book may be reproduced without the publisher's written permission.

Bible quotations, unless otherwise noted, are from the *New Revised Standard Version Bible,* copyright 1989, Division of Christian Education of the National Council of the Churches of Christ in the United States of America. Used by permission. All rights reserved.

Scripture quotations marked (NIV) are taken from the HOLY BIBLE, NEW INTERNATIONAL VERSION®. NIV®. Copyright © 1973, 1978, 1984 by International Bible Society. Used by permission of Zondervan Publishing House. All rights reserved.

Scripture quotations marked CEB are from the Common English Bible., copyright ©2011 by Common English Bible.

Cover art: ©Shutterstock

Print: 9780827231290
EPDF (read-only): 9780827231313   EPUB: 9780827231306

Candlelighting services available at ChalicePress.com
Spend a little family or private time in worship this Advent.
Go to ChalicePress.com, search for or click on
Partners in Prayer 2015, **and follow the link to**
free, downloadable candlelighting services.

"Sing a New Song"

The Advent season is exciting, anticipatory, and contemplative all at the same time. Amid the busyness of the secular Christmas season, as the Church, we take moments to breathe and remember that this season is not yet Christmas, but Advent. Advent means "to arrive" a time to participate in rituals that prepare our hearts, minds, and souls for the birth of the Christ-child.

The theme for this year's devotional is "Sing a New Song." Psalm 98, from which these words come, speaks of the whole earth joining in greeting the promised messiah. During the season of Advent, God's people are called to learn new songs and to hear old songs in new ways, both as faithful individuals and as faith communities.

We take the songs of scripture as our texts for this Advent devotional. Each day readers are invited to read a short passage of scripture and to reflect on those passages using a brief meditation written by a member of The Young Clergy Women Project. The scriptures and themes are primarily drawn from the Revised Common Lectionary Sunday texts and the accompanying daily lectionary.

Each week draws an additional theme from Psalm 98. Week One, "The Reign of God is Near" (Nov. 29–Dec. 5), reminds us to seek God right where we are. Week Two, "The Breaking Dawn" (Dec. 6–12), presents us with ways we are enticed to praise God with song. Week Three, "The Joy of Salvation" (Dec. 13–19), encourages us to embrace what God has done for us and respond with joy. Week Four, "The Great Reversal" (Dec. 20–25), sends the message that God has made us righteous through Christ.

We have also provided prayers for the lighting of Advent candles. These prayers are designed to be used either at home or within the context of a congregational worship service.

Our twenty-seven authors hail from many parts of the United States and world, and they represent a range of denominations. It is our joy to present reflections from many backgrounds and people. We pray that you will grow in faithfulness through this season and with this devotional.

Let the floods clap their hands; let the hills sing together for joy
 at the presence of the LORD, for he is coming to judge the earth.
He will judge the world with righteousness,
 and the peoples with equity. (Psalm 98:8–9)

May God bless you and keep you this Advent season.

REV. APRIL BERENDS, REV. EMILY BROWN,
REV. BRENDA LOVICK, REV. KELLY BOUBEL SHRIVER

Editors of *Partners in Prayer 2015,* The Young Clergy Women Project Board

SUN • NOV 29

For You I Wait

Read Psalm 25:1–10.

...for you are the God of my salvation;
  for you I wait all day long. (Psalm 25:5b)

"You have been waiting an unexpectedly long time...," the letter from our adoption agency read. When it arrived we weren't surprised. My partner and I have been waiting for two years.

Naively, when our adoption journey began, I assumed I would meet our child within a matter of months. A year went by, and then two. I'd like to say I've grown comfortable with waiting, but that's simply not true. There is an edginess to it—an anxiety–filled with questions, apprehension, and nerves. There are moments I breathe into it, allowing myself to trust that my family will take shape in time, but these moments of calm are few.

Yet the reign of God is near. This is the promise of Advent, of our faith. This season challenges us anew to release our anxiety, our fear, and the nerves we carry as we navigate the unknown. Advent invites us to breathe into the waiting, centering ourselves on the abundant grace of God's future in-breaking. This is my adoption task. It is our Advent task. It is holy, beautiful, sacred work.

Prayer: Holy One, as we settle into the waiting, may it be your Spirit that surrounds us, your peace that encompasses us, and your love that sustains us. Amen.

REV. JAMIE HASKINS

MON • NOV 30

Nemesis Song

Read Psalm 19.

*Let the words of my mouth
and the meditations of my heart
be pleasing to you,
Lord, my rock and my redeemer. (Psalm 19:14, CEB)*

"I wish I had earplugs," I grumble as the Christmas song I detest blares cheekily over the sound system. Every holiday season I dread that melody.

We probably all have them: Christmas songs we dislike because of the bad lyrics, the constant repetition, or the memories the song holds. Every year it feels as if my nemesis song is the *only* one that plays. In the midst of this noise, how am I to keep my heart and mind focused on God's work in the world this Advent season?

For I know that God's work is everywhere, as the psalmist reminds us. The skies display it without words, and God's instructions can guide our lives in amazing and surprising ways. Yet we often find ourselves on the path of distraction: grumbling about music, spending more than we can afford, stressing to make everything "perfect," and forgetting to look for God right where we are.

Our challenge on this Advent journey, as we catch ourselves grumbling and anxious, is to breathe deeply and pray, "May the words of my mouth and the meditations of my heart be acceptable in your sight, O God, because you are our strength and redeemer."

Prayer: Re-center me, O God. Open my eyes to see your at work in the world. Open my ears to hear your voice, even amidst the noise and distractions. Amen.

Rev. Diana Hodges-Batzka

TUE • DEC 1

Dust to Dust, Everlasting to Everlasting

Read Psalm 90:1–6.

*Lord, you have been our dwelling place
in all generations.
Before the mountains were brought forth,
or ever you had formed the earth and the world,
from everlasting to everlasting you are God. (Psalm 90:1–2)*

I was thirteen when I realized just how small I was in the "big picture." I wasn't given to theological reflection; I spent my days swooning over the boy who sat next to me in band. But one day my science teacher gave an off-curriculum lecture about the scope and history of the universe. The unfathomable size and age of the world flabbergasted me. I had a fleeting glimpse of my fleeting existence. It was disturbing. (I must have recovered swiftly, because my next vivid memory was receiving my first kiss from the band boy, and I am quite sure I wasn't still in the midst of an existential crisis.)

We are small. We inhabit the tiniest sliver of time and space. In the grand scheme of things, one could argue that any given life is insignificant. But one would be wrong. We may be dust to dust, but God is our dwelling place, and God is vast and ancient—everlasting to everlasting.

Prayer: Let us be humble and joyful in your presence, O God, as your reign draws near. Amen.

REV. KATHERINE WILLIS PERSHEY

WED • DEC 2

Our Days Are Numbered

Read Psalm 90:12–17.

Teach us to number our days,...
[E]stablish the work of our hands... (Psalm 90:12a, 17b, NIV)

As a child of the church, I was terrified by the end of the world. It sounded so scary that I would lie awake at nights, fearful for my soul and for the world I loved. I couldn't imagine ever praying, "*Maranatha*, come Lord Jesus," with real eagerness.

Now, as a pastor and an adult, I still lie awake some nights fearful for my soul and for the world I love. Only now I am fearful that Christ is not returning quickly enough. I fear that, in the interim, famine and war and my own selfishness are damaging the world I love. I am eager for the blessing of the infant Jesus we celebrate at Christmas to reach "far as the curse is found."

Our work of preparation, then, is to align our hearts and our lives to the Kingdom God has promised. "May God bless you and the work of your hands," is one of the earliest recorded blessings of the church. It is a prayer of preparation and eagerness for the day when all things will be made right.

Prayer: God of Christmas and Kingdom, prepare our hearts for your reign. By your Spirit, may the work of our hands align our lives to the wholeness You have promised. In Jesus' name we pray. Amen.

REV. MEG JENISTA

THUR • DEC 3

Resounding Gratitude

Read 1 Thessalonians 3:9–13.

And may the Lord make you increase and abound in love for one another and for all, just as we abound in love for you.
(1 Thessalonians 3:12)

Gratitude is a hallmark of Paul's first letter to the Thessalonians. "We always give thanks to God for all of you and mention you in our prayers," the letter begins, culminating five chapters later with, "Rejoice always, pray without ceasing, give thanks in all circumstances; for this is the will of God in Christ Jesus for you" (1:2, 5:16–18).

While it was customary for Paul and his contemporaries to bookend their letters with expressions of thanksgiving, 1 Thessalonians stands apart; gratitude resounds throughout the epistle. In today's reading from the heart of the third chapter, we hear Paul's deep thanksgiving for the continued faithfulness of those who will hear his words. "How can we thank God enough for you?" asks Paul, adding, "Night and day we pray most earnestly that we may see you face to face" (3:9–10).

How might gratitude accompany our Advent journey as we long to see Jesus face to face?

Prayer: O God who was, and is, and is to come, during this expectant season, make us truly grateful for the promise of the child in the manger. By your faithfulness, transform our gratitude into acts of justice, mercy, and abundant love for one another and for all. Amen.

REV. AUSTIN CRENSHAW SHELLEY

FRI • DEC 4

Comfort Comes Softly

Read Isaiah 40:1-11.

*Comfort, O comfort my people,
says your God. (Isaiah 40:1)*

Last winter I sat in the waiting room of the county hospital's surgical ward. Early in the morning we checked in for my partner's outpatient procedure, claiming a spot in the corner next to the magazine pile: *Bassmaster, O, Time*. We waited, and we waited. They finally called her name.

I'd prayed with people as a hospital chaplain, but it was my first time on this side of surgery. It felt institutional, anonymous. Cracker crumbs littered the floor, even at 6 a.m. A disconcerting number of upholstered chairs had visible stains. Men in hard hats and well-worn jeans walked through. It was not comforting.

Minutes passed. Hours. My phone dinged with a new text message: *How are you? How's Jamie?* I responded. Then another ding, another person from another corner of life. Then again and again. One of my sisters called to tell me about her new purse. After we hung up I realized she was really checking on me, and Jamie. My in-laws sent a picture of a tomato plant knowing I'm an avid gardener. I realized they were checking, too.

Comfort came softly: the easing of the waiting, the subtle declaration of love's presence. As is often the case, comfort was nearer than I realized. So was the Divine, gathering me there in her arms.

Prayer: Holy One, you are near whether we know it or not. Comfort us. Amen.

REV. SARAH KLAASSEN

SAT · DEC 5

Share in God's Grace with Me

Read Philippians 1:1–13.

"It is right for me to think this way about all of you, because you hold me in your heart, for all of you share in God's grace with me, both in my imprisonment and in the defense and confirmation of the gospel." (Philippians 1:7)

Several years ago, I joined a fitness community in which the instructor encouraged everyone to share not only their fitness and life goals, but also ten daily "gratitudes" via e-mail as a means of cultivating a positive focus on life. The response was almost overwhelming, and the instructor observed the community springing to life with mutual support, shared gratitude, and heartfelt encouragement. When she herself went through a difficult separation and the tragic death of a family member, the community the instructor helped to build surrounded and supported her. This was a powerful testimony to the importance of a community in bearing life's ups and downs.

This is the spirit in which Paul writes to the community of Christians in Philippi, where believers had encouraged him in times of both great sorrow and great joy. Paul reminds us how a person can be lifted up simply by knowing he or she is not alone. As we prepare for Jesus' Incarnation, God calls us to consider the ways in which we live as Christ's body in the world, as communities that encourage our members in the truth of God's redeeming love.

Prayer: O God, hold me close through this day. No matter where I am, give me courage to see your presence. Amen.

REV. JULIE M. HOPLAMAZIAN

SUN • DEC 6

What's in a Name?

Read Luke 1:57–66.

All who heard them pondered them and said, "What then will this child become?" For, indeed, the hand of the Lord was with him. (Luke 1:66)

What's in a name? In earlier times and in a variety of cultures, names were words of power; they often signified family legacies or described what type of personality the child would have. In contemporary culture, many people use names as expressions of individuality, choosing unusual names and creative spellings of classic names, without as much emphasis on a connection to the familial as there was in John's time. Therefore, it is easy to overlook the gravity and strangeness of Elizabeth and Zechariah's actions when they did not follow the typical naming procedure. As we discover so often in the scriptures, God may have other plans.

When we receive our names, they are signs of belonging and identity. "What then will this child become?" can be asked of us at our birth and when we join our Christian community. No matter what our parents name us or what we call ourselves, in becoming Christ's own forever, we gain a truer name: *beloved.*

What then, should our response to our naming be? In claiming our identity as "beloved," what then will we become?

Prayer: Divine Creator, you are known by many names. In this moment, remind me of my true name and give me the courage to become the person you have created me to be. Amen.

REV. DANÁE ASHLEY

MON • DEC 7

Out of the Mouths

Read Luke 1:68–71.

"As [God] spoke through the mouth of [the] holy prophets from of old, that we would be saved..." (Luke 1:70–71a)

"Mom! Mom!" My five-year-old is constantly seeking my attention—especially when I'm trying to sustain a conversation with another adult. And, I'll be honest, his comments are usually, well...let's be charitable and call them trivial. Often, I end up feeling frustrated at the interruption.

My sons are named for great prophets of our tradition: Enoch, Moses, Jonah. Sometimes their names alone are enough of a reminder for me to stop and listen: to hear their words with the same care I give to the words of those great prophets; to look them in the eyes; to hear precisely what they're trying to tell me; to listen to their stories. While the stories are, yes, usually trivial, the interactions are not. And, on rare occasions, their "kid" questions present a gift: a new way to see the world.

God speaks through the mouths gathered around us, if we have ears to hear—to hear the prophecies of the old, the concerns of the young, the stories of our people. In those stories, I wonder what we'll find? Maybe a new way to see the world?

Prayer: Gracious God, you are still speaking to us. Open our ears to hear your words from the voices gathered all around. Amen.

REV. KELLY BOUBEL SHRIVER

TUE • DEC 8

Salvation in Forgiveness

Read Luke 1:72–77.

*"And you, child, will be called the prophet of the Most High;
for you will go before the Lord to prepare his ways,
to give knowledge of salvation to his people
by the forgiveness of their sins." (Luke 1:76–77)*

    Zechariah, the father of newborn John, can finally speak again after nine months of silence. He envisions the future for his son: prophecy, salvation, forgiveness of sins. God breaks Zechariah's silence to proclaim that God is doing a long-awaited new thing.

    Many can relate to the agony Zechariah has seen in his life. Sadness, anger, and fear permeate a world characterized by broken lives, hopeless relationships, divided communities, and nations torn apart. We live in a world that needs to be saved again and again.

    Zechariah's baby brings hope to this world. He will be known as John the Baptist, because he will understand God's intention for creation. This new life points us to Jesus, who releases us from our brokenness and frees us to live into God's love. As our words and actions show God's gracious love, our lives also point to Jesus. Trusting and hoping in Christ, our lives in faith manifest God's forgiveness to a broken world. Zechariah's hope for us is that God-in-flesh reveals a better way.

Prayer: Most High, guide us in forgiveness so that your salvific love may break into our world and prepare the way of the Christ-child. Amen.

REV. BRENDA LOVICK

WED • DEC 9

Dawn from on High

Read Luke 1:78-79.

*"By the tender mercy of our God,
the dawn from on high will break upon us." (Luke 1:78)*

Every morning during the darker months of the year, I sit in front of a "happy lamp" while I eat breakfast. This lamp mimics sunlight, counteracting the effects of reduced daylight on mood and emotions. I've always struggled with depression during the winter, and the happy lamp has made a dramatic difference for me since I started using it a few years ago. When the days are shortest, I often get up before it's light out, so the happy lamp is like my own artificial dawn.

The lamp helps get me through the dark days, but it is nothing compared to the real thing. As the days lengthen, and the dawn comes earlier and earlier, I begin to anticipate the day when there will be enough true sunlight to sustain me and I can put away the lamp for another year.

When Christ comes into our lives, it is like the dawn finally breaking after long years of living by artificial light. Many other kinds of light may ease the darkness for us, but there is no replacement for the true Light of the world.

Prayer: God of tenderness, shine your love into our hearts, and help us to share your Light with others. Amen.

REV. DIANA CARROLL

THUR • DEC 10

The Promise of Hope

Read Isaiah 35:3–7.

Then the eyes of the blind shall be opened... (Isaiah 35:5a)

She attended worship every Sunday with her trusted assistance dog. The forty-something woman had been blind since birth. One Sunday I overheard another parishioner asking her about the scripture I had read. "Does it upset you to hear things like that? All the talk about the blind being able to see?" The blind woman seemed perplexed. "Why would that message bother me? There's hope in those words! Don't you believe what it says?"

That is a good question for us to ponder: Do *we* believe? Do we believe Isaiah's prophetic words of promise? Do we believe these words are meant for *us*?

When the people heard these words, they were living in exile. God spoke a message of hope to them, promising that *they will be saved.* Many of us have struggled in "exile" in our own lives. We have endured abuse, stress, unemployment, cancer, and depression. God's message of hope comes to us, too: We will be saved! God *will* break into our lives, transforming bleak into beautiful, dull into dazzling, and hopeless into hopeful. The question is: Do we believe what God says?

Prayer: Holy One, awaken us to your powerful promise of hope. Break into our lives as living water. Free us to see and hear and dance and sing to the glory of your name! Amen.

REV. AMY LOVING AUSTIN

FRI • DEC 11

Joy in the Harvest

Read Psalm 126.

May those who sow in tears
reap with shouts of joy. (Psalm 126:5)

One fall I cried while planting bulbs in the ground following one of my most difficult years of ministry. I was not even sure I would still be living in the same place when the bulbs bloomed. Yet, I could skip neither the ritual, nor the promise that at the end of a long winter the dawn would come earlier and the bulbs would emerge. That spring, I was there to see the beginnings of leaves peeking up through the dirt. When they were tall enough, I cut a bouquet of tulips for my table as a reminder that God had once again kept the promise that new life would come.

This psalm reminds us that the God who was faithful to the people of Israel in the past will be faithful in the years to come. Those who sow with tears will find joy in the harvest. The tears that watered the bulbs resulted in blooms that signaled God's promise. In this midwinter season, God is at work. As the days grow shorter and the dawn arrives later, may we hold fast to the promises that God will help us reap with joy.

Prayer: God of Creation, as the dawn breaks on this new day, help us to look forward to the day when the dawn breaks over the manger holding your Son. Amen.

REV. JULIE JENSEN

SAT • DEC 12

Our Warrior for Justice

Read Zephaniah 3:14–20.

*The LORD, your God, is in your midst,
    a warrior who gives victory;
he will rejoice over you with gladness,
    he will renew you in his love;
he will exult over you with loud singing
    as on a day of festival. (Zephaniah 3:17–18a)*

In the Disney film *Mulan*, the title character struggles to find her true identity. She poses the question to herself: "When will my reflection show who I am inside?" Through the help of companions on her journey, she not only becomes a warrior and a heroine, she also discovers who she is, and her family is able to celebrate with her.

Each of us have people who help us break free from the confines society imposes on us to become the people God wants us to become. In Zephaniah, God rejoices over the people like a victorious warrior, just as we have people who see our potential, cheer us on, and celebrate our victories. This day I remember my great-uncle, who campaigned for women's ordination and was instrumental in allowing my reflection to show who I am inside.

Prayer: Ever-loving God, our eternal warrior for justice: We celebrate the light that breaks through the dawn of oppression and injustice. We give thanks this day for those who encourage, inspire, and guide us into becoming the individuals God created us to be. In the name of the Source of all life and the Spirit of love, Amen.

REV. SARAH LAMMING

SUN • DEC 13

Singing When You're Afraid

Read Isaiah 12:2–6.

Surely God is my salvation;
I will trust, and will not be afraid... (Isaiah 12:2)

I come from a family of singers. Mom is the lyric soprano, sister the alto, brother the bass, dad the baritone, and I'm the bonus soprano. I grew up singing for every possible occasion; there's even a "Take Out the Trash" song.

But do you know when it's really hard to sing? When you're afraid. When life is terrible. When the tragedies come so fast and so furious that it's difficult to breathe, let alone hum the bridge of the latest Katy Perry pop song. When you can't sing, you still crave the melodies. So, you listen for voices who can sing to you in the midst of your silence. Or at least I did.

When my life crumbled into ash and I lost my songs, I stumbled back upon the truth-bearing melody of God and found verses to speak to my wounded soul. Songs such as Isaiah's, words of hope in the midst of destruction and exile: "*Surely God is my salvation; I will...not be afraid.*" The promise of Isaiah, the promise of Advent, is that the song continues, salvation comes, no matter if you are afraid or how long the dark night lingers. Rejoice and sing, dear ones, for *"he has become...salvation" (Isaiah 12:2d).*

Prayer: Sing us the song again, Loving God—the song of hope, of salvation. Sing it to us until we are no longer afraid. Amen.

REV. ELIZABETH GRASHAM

MON • DEC 14

Rejoice Reminder

Philippians 4:4–7.

Rejoice in the Lord always; again I will say, Rejoice. (Philippians 4:4)

    The apostle Paul seems to think that the Philippians need a "Rejoice Reminder." He tells them not once, but twice, to rejoice in the Lord, adding emphasis and perhaps even giving permission for these followers of Christ to celebrate joy. In the midst of broken hearts, bodies, and communities, we, too, could use a Rejoice Reminder. But what does joy in the Lord look like?

    One of my first assignments for *Church Health Reader* was interviewing Fr. Jim Martin, author of the book *Between Heaven and Mirth*, in which he distinguishes joy from happiness. Happiness is wonderful but often fleeting. Joy is rooted in our relationship with God. It is that joy that enables us to relish in the resurrection even in the midst of grief, or to embrace that nervous laughter before receiving the diagnosis. Joy is not always a happy feeling, but the deeper happiness of knowing God was, is, and always shall be, our peace.

Prayer: God who surpasses our understanding, we present our requests to you; trusting in your peace, living in your gentleness, rejoicing in your love, we pray. Amen.

Rev. Stacy Smith

TUE • DEC 15

Snap Judgment

Read Isaiah 11:1–5.

*"He shall not judge by what his eyes see,
or decide by what his ears hear…" (Isaiah 11:3b)*

    Earlier this year, it was a dress that was blue and black (or white and gold), an escaped llama, and the Kardashians. The next month, it was Michelle Obama's hairstyle, legislation in Indiana, and the Kardashians. By the time you read this, it will be something else entirely…although still probably the Kardashians.

    We live in a culture of click bait and sound bites. News stories become history almost before they become public. We form quick opinions, trade witty remarks, and move on to the next trending topic. It's fun, and it gives us something to do on social media. But this same culture can be unforgiving. It teaches us to see things in black and white, to move toward quick laughs instead of compassion, to be harsh and judgmental. It can be terribly cruel, as you know if you've ever been on the wrong end of the rumor mill.

    Thankfully, God's judgment is not the snap judgment of contemporary "infotainment." Scripture promises One who will judge not on appearances and sound bites, but with righteousness; One who will look not at the surface, but the heart…and that is good and joyful news for everyone—even the Kardashians. Even us.

Prayer: Righteous and merciful God, look with kindness upon us, your frequently judgmental people, and teach us to do the same. Amen.

Rev. Emily Brown

WED • DEC 16

Mortal Danger?

Read Isaiah 11:6–9.

*The wolf shall live with the lamb,
the leopard shall lie down with the kid,...
and a little child shall lead them. (Isaiah 11:6)*

In our dog-eat-dog world, Isaiah echoes through the centuries, offering a promise of idyllic harmony. However, anyone who has ever watched a documentary about the natural world knows very well that some animals are predators and others prey.

Isaiah paints a striking picture. Not only will predator and prey live in life-giving relationship, but an innocent child is center stage. Places of deadly danger—the den of the adder—will be transformed into places of wholeness. Isaiah speaks of a vision beyond our wildest imagination. Perhaps that is the point.

In Advent, we look to a time with God so different from that which we find familiar, we cannot imagine it. The only way we can comprehend it is through impossible icons of wolf and lamb, of leopard with kid, of child and adder. To his original reader, the images Isaiah spun represented mortal danger. Might we ponder, What images in our world represent mortal danger? Where are the places we might wish to see so transformed that a child might safely play?

Prayer: World-bending God, the future you promise is beyond our wildest imagination. We struggle to picture what fullness of life with you could be like. Enable us to glimpse this; help us not discount the vision as impossible. Amen.

REV. SARAH MOORE

THUR • DEC 17

Turning the Page

Psalm 51:1-15.

Create a clean heart for me, God;
put a new, faithful spirit deep inside me!
Please don't throw me out of your presence;
please don't take your holy spirit away from me.
Return the joy of your salvation to me
and sustain me with a willing spirit. (Psalm 51:10-12, CEB)

    This is the time of year I think about fresh starts and clean slates. Perhaps it has something to do with all the memories that come rushing back during this season of family gatherings, office parties, and Christmas cards. I think about how I should reconnect with this family member or that. I wonder about mistakes I've made once upon a time or, sometimes, yesterday. I mull over those broken places and missing pieces.

    David and I are kindred spirits this time of year. In Psalm 51 we hear David praying for a new beginning, a fresh start. He prays for God to forgive his sins of yesterday, which are many. Thankfully for David, and for us, we pray to a God of steadfast love and abundant mercy. During this season of preparation, let us open our hearts to God's cleansing work, for it is through our Lord's love that we receive wholeness and new beginnings.

Prayer: God of Wonder, thank you for the gift of second chances. We offer up to you our lackluster joy and halfhearted spirit. Place us on your path to salvation. Amen.

REV. SARAH GLADSTONE

FRI • DEC 18

Salvation from Fear

Read Isaiah 51.

*You fear continually all day long
because of the fury of the oppressor...
But where is the fury of the oppressor? (Isaiah 51:13b)*

Advent points to the coming joy of Christ. Advent also demands we take stock of a world desperately in need of Emmanuel, God with us. Nestled in Isaiah's prophecy of joy and gladness, we find a harsh but honest assessment of the state of nations, communities, and our very souls.

Whether we live under political oppression, systemic discrimination, the weight of depression, anxiety, addiction, or myriad nameless torments known only in our own hearts, our world thrives on fear. Fear stops our ears from hearing good news. Fear blinds our eyes to beauty and wonder. Fear robs us of hope. Fear portrays itself as the way of the world. But then we hear Isaiah's song—a song of memory when ours fail, a song of gladness amid comfortless circumstance, and a song of salvation.

Whatever fear holds us captive, God will release us. However scared or weak we feel, God will help us stand. Fear need not be the way of the world. Christ is coming. With Isaiah, let us sing in joy.

Prayer: Holy One, drive fear from our hearts. Let joy and gladness reign. Remind us that you are Lord, whose promise is true, and you are with us always. Amen.

REV. PHYLLIS L. STUTZMAN

SAT • DEC 19

Finding the Center

Read Psalm 113.

[God] lifts the needy from the ash heap. (Psalm 113:7b, NIV)

I went to the labyrinth because I was deeply wounded and in need of healing. At other times in my life, I'd taken the journey to the center and found peace...answers...a word from God.

Labyrinths aren't mazes. If you stay on the path, there's only one way in and one way out. It's impossible to get lost. Yet, on that day of deep grief and confusion, I wasn't paying attention. My mind was trapped in its own maze of tortured thoughts, and I stepped into the wrong pathway. Instead of journeying to the center, I had turned around and was heading back out, having missed the center completely. When I reached the entrance I ran away, embarrassed and crying. It felt like I was being expelled from the kingdom, a complete and total failure. I ran to a tree nearby where I cried and wondered why God would allow me to take the wrong path at a time when I needed God the most.

I'm really trying here, I thought, as the tears kept falling. And then, mercifully, the Spirit's peace washed over me. *I'm not only in the center,* God was saying, *I'm on the edges too. I'm here, under this tree. You don't have to do it right. Just sit.*

Prayer: Loving God, thank you for being present in the center and on the edges. Thank you for finding me and meeting me where I am. Amen.

Rev. Traci Smith

SUN • DEC 20

The Song of the Least

Read Micah 5:2–5a.

"But you, O Bethlehem of Ephrathah,
  who are one of the little clans of Judah,
from you shall come forth for me
  one who is to rule in Israel…" (Micah 5:2a)

As we near the end of Advent, many of us are preparing for a warm celebration with friends and family members. We've made our houses festive; we're finishing up our shopping. Christmas often comes with a sense of completion.

The longing and anticipation of Advent won't wrap up as the presents come undone on December 25. Micah reminds us that the long-expected one comes to backwater places, to people whom the world has forgotten. The prophet speaks to Israel during a time in which her own leaders collaborated with her oppressors, systematizing injustice and further crushing those who lived in poverty. Salvation, says the prophet, will come not from the center of power in Jerusalem, but from the little town of Bethlehem, home of shepherds.

The one for whom we're waiting doesn't just come to the cozy places, the living rooms with lighted trees or churches decked with fragrant greens and gleaming candles. He comes to people who are enraged, to neighborhoods torn apart, to people who grieve, to people whose bodies are giving out. He comes to a world that needs a savior.

Prayer: O God, you lift up those who are the least among us. Transform their cries into our song, that we may respond with Christ's own love. Amen.

REV. APRIL BERENDS

MON • DEC 21

Responding to Reversal

Read Luke 1:46b–49.

*"My soul magnifies the Lord,
  and my spirit rejoices in God my Savior,
for he has looked with favor on the lowliness of his servant.
  Surely, from now on all generations will call me blessed;
for the Mighty One has done great things for me,
  and holy is his name."*
(Luke 1:46b–49)

Mary reacts to the plans God is bringing to life through her in a surprisingly positive way. Her soul takes a closer look, makes God a bigger centerpiece in her already faithful life, and her spirit rejoices. The tiny heartbeat and little moving arms and legs growing within her are all part of an event she chooses to receive as a blessing.

How often in moments of uncertainty have we chosen to respond by magnifying the Lord, by seeing the blessings, by rejoicing in how God saves?

As we prepare to receive anew the God who arrives through great reversals, let us consider our responses to God's action in our lives and in the world. When shock and displeasure are our gut reactions to an event, how might we see a blessing, or suspend judgment to await the great things God reveals in upheaval?

Prayer: Mighty One, I want to magnify you and rejoice in your saving grace. Open my heart and transform my vision, that I may see and respond to your goodness at work in all things. Amen.

REV. ELAINE MURRAY DREEBEN

TUE • DEC 22

A Song in the Darkness

Read Isaiah 9:2–7.

*The people who walked in darkness
   have seen a great light;
those who lived in a land of deep darkness—
   on them light has shined...*

*For a child has been born for us,
   a son given to us;
authority rests upon his shoulders;
   and he is named
Wonderful Counselor... (Isaiah 9:2, 6)*

    Walking through the valley of the shadow of mental illness is often a lonely road. Depression feels like a time of deep darkness, a time when God is nowhere to be found.
    Isaiah wants us to know that this darkness we feel is only temporary. Light is coming. But we have to seek out help; we have to break the silence about mental illness for the light to be able to break in.
    We can take deep comfort trusting that the One who brings the world's greatest hope, the One who is Light in the darkness, Isaiah nicknames "Wonderful Counselor." When we realize we cannot walk through this life alone, our Wonderful Counselor teaches us how to sing a new song.

Prayer: Wonderful Counselor, help all who live with mental illness and their loved ones find hope. We give thanks that in sharing our sorrows and troubles with a trusted person, we can learn to sing a new song. Amen.

REV. SARAH LUND

WED • DEC 23

The Call of the *Magnificat*

Read Luke 1:52–55.

*"He has brought down the powerful from their thrones,
   and lifted up the lowly;
he has filled the hungry with good things,
   and sent the rich away empty.*

*He has helped his servant Israel,
   in remembrance of his mercy,
according to the promise he made to our ancestors,
   to Abraham and to his descendants for ever." (Luke 1:52–55)*

While studying in England, I heard this passage on an almost daily basis. In the Anglican tradition, the *Magnificat* (Luke 1:46–55) is said or sung as the response to the readings during evening worship. Hearing these remarkable words sung by children and adults as I sat in the choir stalls of one of England's magnificent cathedrals was a true gift. I was moved by the beauty of the place and the sounds, and the daily repetition of the *Magnificat* has stayed with me. It taught me that the *Magnificat* is always a good idea. Whatever scripture we might hear, the *Magnificat* is always an appropriate response. We need to perennially be reminded that God is on the side of the powerless, the hungry, the poor, the needy. If we are to follow Jesus, that is where we should be too. We need a daily reminder that our calling is to speak truth to power and lift up the lowly.

Prayer: Lord, call us to your side, to be champions of justice and agents of your restoring and reconciling love in the world. Amen.

REV. MOLLY F. JAMES

THUR • DEC 24

Advantage Humility

Read Luke 1:50–51.

*"His mercy is for those who fear him
from generation to generation.*

*He has shown strength with his arm;
he has scattered the proud in the thoughts of their hearts."*
(Luke 1:50–51)

    We know that God is compassionate and merciful. Because God cares intimately about our lives and all of creation, and because God has made such efforts in Christ to draw near to us, we can know God as "father" in a meaningful way. All of this allows for a remarkable relationship between humans and God, one in which we can not only share our joys and secret hopes, but also in which we can reveal our deep doubts and disappointments.

    As wonderful as this is, we must remember that even though God is very close to us, God is still *God*, and "other" than us. God deserves respect and, in the sense of the word that means awe and admiration, fear. God's mercy and compassion become most real to us when we recognize just how far God knelt in order to reach out to us.

Prayer: God, help us to remember that those who are humble have an unseen and unbeatable advantage—the love and refuge of a God who honors and defends the humble. Amen.

REV. KELSEY GRISSOM

FRI • DEC 25

A Roaring Peace

Read Psalm 98.

Let the sea roar, and all that fills it;
  the world and those who live in it. (Psalm 98:7)

Imagine the perfect early Christmas morning: outside, a snow-muffled world while you sit inside with a warm mug of something and bask in the lights of the tree before the rush of presents, family, friends, and feasting. On a day when we celebrate the birth of a baby, such a quiet, tender beginning to contemplate new life couldn't be more appropriate, could it?

Unless, as Psalm 98 suggests, a raw ocean wind and the continual call and response of surf pounding the sand is a better wake-up call on this marvelous day.

It's easy to get caught up in the sweetness of the newborn baby Jesus, and forget that contained in those tiny fingers and toes is the entirety of God-with-us. The miracle of Christmas is not peace in the sense of quiet. It is peace in the sense of wholeness, that the Lord of all creation has come to live among us, and set the world right.

Prayer: Lord of all creation, tune my heart to sing with the whole world on this most marvelous day. With trees and hills, rivers and oceans, and all people everywhere, may I sing with joy for the promise of your great peace. Amen.

REV. ERICA L. SCHEMPER

CONTRIBUTORS

Rev. Danáe Ashley is the associate priest for St. Stephen's Episcopal Church, Seattle, Washington, and is also becoming a licensed marriage and family therapist.

Rev. Amy E. Loving Austin is the pastor of Seneca Presbyterian Church and Bellona Memorial Presbyterian Church in the Finger Lakes region of upstate New York.

Rev. April Berends is an Episcopal priest serving in the Diocese of Tennessee.

Rev. Emily M. Brown is the associate pastor of Broadway United Church of Christ in New York City.

Rev. Diana Carroll is the rector of St. Luke's Episcopal Church in Annapolis and chaplain at St. Anne's School of Annapolis.

Rev. Elaine Murray Dreeben is the pastor of Canyon Lake Presbyterian Church, Canyon Lake, Texas.

Rev. Sarah Gladstone is the pastor of Hampshire Colony Congregational Church in Princeton, Illinois.

Rev. Elizabeth Grasham is the senior minister at Heights Christian Church (Disciples of Christ), in Houston, Texas.

Rev. Kelsey Grissom is the associate pastor of Asbury United Methodist Church in Birmingham, Alabama.

Rev. Jamie Haskins serves as chaplain at Westminster College, Fulton, Missouri.

Rev. Diana Hodges-Batzka serves as Associate Minister at Florence Christian Church (Disciples of Christ) in Florence, Kentucky.

The Reverend Julie M. Hoplamazian is the associate rector of Grace Church Brooklyn Heights (Episcopal).

Rev. Molly F. James, Ph.D. serves as dean of formation for the Episcopal Church in Connecticut and co-chair of The Young Clergy Women Project.

Rev. Meg Jenista is pastor at The Washington, D.C., Christian Reformed Church.

Rev. Julie Jensen is the associate pastor for Congregational Care and Mission at First Presbyterian Church in Cartersville, Georgia.

Rev. Sarah Klaassen is a community organizer and pastor in Columbia, Missouri.

Rev. Sarah Lamming is an Episcopal priest in the Diocese of Maryland.

Rev. Brenda Lovick, LMFT, is pastor of the historic Norwegian American congregation East Koshkonong Lutheran Church in rural Cambridge, Wisconsin.

Rev. Dr. Sarah Griffith Lund is the author of *Blessed Are the Crazy: Breaking the Silence about Mental Illness, Family, and Church* (Chalice Press, 2014). Sarah serves on the leadership teams of Christian Theological Seminary, the Bethany Ecumenical Fellows, and the United Church of Christ Mental Health Network. She blogs at www.sarahgriffithlund.com.

Rev. Sarah Moore is president of the Cumbria Area of the North Western Synod of the United Reformed Church, United Kingdom.

Rev. Katherine Willis Pershey is an associate minister of First Congregational Church of Western Springs, Illinois. She is the author of *Any Day a Beautiful Change: A Story of Faith and Family* (Chalice Press, 2012).

Rev. Erica L. Schemper is a PC(USA) minister and the director of children, youth, and family ministries at Holy Trinity Lutheran Church in San Carlos, California.

Rev. Austin Crenshaw Shelley serves as associate pastor for Christian education at The Presbyterian Church of Chestnut Hill in Philadelphia, Pennsylvania.

Rev. Kelly Boubel Shriver is head of staff at Peoples Presbyterian Church in Milan, Michigan, and also the co-chair of The Young Clergy Women Project.

Rev. Stacy Smith is editor of *Church Health Reader* and director of knowledge ministry at the Church Health Center in Memphis, Tennessee. She is the author of *Bless Her Heart: Life as a Young Clergy Woman* (Chalice Press, 2011).

Rev. Traci Smith is pastor of Northwood Presbyterian Church, San Antonio, and author of *Seamless Faith: Simple Practices for Daily Family Life* (Chalice Press, 2014). Contact her at www.traci-smith.com.

Rev. Phyllis L. Stutzman pastors First Presbyterian Church in Tecumseh, Oklahoma.

The Young Clergy Women Project is a professional network of the youngest ordained clergy women, defined as those under forty. With more than 1,500 members, we live across the United States and around the world, and represent more than two dozen denominations.

We gather whenever and wherever we can—regionally, at denominational events, at an annual conference, and online. TYCWP publishes new, fresh, and evocative articles written by members of our community on our e-zine called *Fidelia's Sisters*, and we have partnered with Chalice Press to publish a book series authored by TYCWP members.

TYCWP seeks to provide members with opportunities for online relationship-building and wisdom-sharing. Our members are invited to share in a password-protected community with other young clergy women on Facebook and on our website. Twitter and Facebook foster this password-protected community and further provide members and friends of TYCWP with the opportunity to catch up on the latest news.

We encourage our members to gather together in their areas for regional meet-ups. We offer support and nurture in-person meet-up gatherings in local churches, at coffee shops, and at denominational events. In these gatherings, our members meet for coffee or a meal and transition their online connections into real-life friendships.

TYCWP also offers community to those young women discerning a call into the ministry. "Future Young Clergy Women" is a password-protected online community for young women waiting for ordination found both on Facebook and on our website.

Learn more about The Young Clergy Women Project online at www.youngclergywomen.org and follow us on Twitter @TYCWP.